Offering

Poems for Peace

Bree M.

Contents

Patchwork

Threads unraveling
from a beautiful quilt
he pulls
she pulls
everyone pulls
they go away
the beauty it once displayed
slowly begins to fade
its strength dispersed among those
who passed through for warmth
now aware of its waning existence
it begs the Maker
to come and mend
its ragged pieces

To Get Back

In and around
the Light abounds
and shines on those
who lost their glow

Second Wind

I felt flattened in my space
people, places, things
had me near expiration
stripped of inspiration
all sense of creativity numbed
everything showing me
that this was it

      but then…

a window opened
and a breeze rushed in
unannounced
yet
unapologetic
it danced down the hairs of my forearm
in an instant
I picked up the pen
the ink pressed into the paper
and breathed life anew

Be Still

If we listen
closely
there is much to be heard
in the
silence

Relations

We are outta line
this time
fed up
broken down
we are not aligned
at this time

Wherever we
went wrong let's
go back to move forward
and carry on
let's
humble
yes
humble ourselves

let's
find our way back
to each other
or let it be
whichever best
leads to peace

What, of a Blackout?

What do we do
when the sun takes a break
but the moon
does not shine either?
Beloved,
we are never
without
for the Light exists
within

Surrender

When unease sweeps in
let Your living waters
overtake me
so that I may float
in the calm
that is You
the working things together for good
that You do
Your compassionate waves
orchestrate my destination
with each push
I rest deeper

The One Who Saves

I rejoice
just to know
that even as
You sit on high
You see as low
as I am
in this moment

        I rejoice
        just to know
        that nothing escapes
        Your view
        nothing escapes
        Your reach
        memories of how
        You lifted me
        time and again
        brings peace within
        as I await
        Your rescue

Clarity

Gone is
the internal battle
that found my mind racing
thoughts in conflict
torn between
this way and that
ever since
I decided
to do things your way
Yahweh
I decided
that on this journey
I will seek you
and find you
on the way
rather than
in the way

Outside Noise

I bagged it
up
and tossed it
back.

All that's left
is
inner voice.

Release

The sun is up
I lay here
joined by peace
staring at quiet
body still
mind busy
thoughts rush forward
urging for freedom
I comply
they spill out
organizing themselves into words
forming lines
a verse
a poem
this poem
I am satisfied

The Ones to Keep

On days
                when
Life groans by like
D train after dark
and Rest chooses recess
I stretch out my arms
and reach way back
                into
summertime heat
in these streets
handball off bricks
in the 'Nam
hydrants spray
on each block
make
                huge splatter
over faces
and sidewalks
fried chicken
and hot butter biscuits
Grandma calls
and
                we scatter

memories
make me
smile wide
'cause
Past brings gifts to
Present
and
                Nothing. Even. Matters.

Morning Glory

Feels like
just before dawn
iridescent glow
tints Black skin
matching sky

Feels like
pounding of hearts
and feet
into rubber particles
could go for miles

Feels like
crossing up wind
before laying up the rock
to sun
we ball

Feels like
moving bodies
at Baisley
get set
we sweat
nothing at all

Mine

Warm bubble bath
drawn up just right
candles lit
I lie
inside
the heat
of the oven baking chocolate chip cookies
that ooze gooey
when you grip
corks to pop bottles
of chilled wine
glasses waiting for the pour
waiting for more
nights like these
to come around more often
music softens
soft skin
closed eyes
I lie
inside
satisfied
this peace…

    It's mine.

A Tall Tree

Find me
under a tall tree
shade as my blanket
unbothered
with the dealings
of life

For Peace's Sake

don't say
they say
pretend
don't show
and after
sealed lips
and fraudulent smiles
hands holding onto
worn out brooms
that for years
swept problems
under rugs
that ripped
we tripped
over
messes made from
dilemmas birthed
voices lost
secrets kept
nothing goes
it lingers there
no one grows
in this collective

so
for peace's sake
run from silence
turn the volume up
loud
on truth
find comfort in
the dis ease
let it be through
spoken words
that we
keep the peace

PSA

If there be peace
let us run straight to it
open arms, plenty spacious
let us run free through it

If there be peace
let us defer to calm
weary souls find rest
idle bodies move on

If there be peace
let us war no more
scars fade to memories
disagreements don't keep score

If there be peace
let us break into song
watch us dance into night
movements waking up dawn

If there be peace
don't sweat what we choose
I can live like me
and you live like you

If there be peace
let my Black be free
keep my bloodline long
let my life just be

If there be peace
let love be too
if there be peace
be it found in you

The Jagged Way

I met living
the moment I decided
to escape perfection's grip
I found peace
the moment I chose
to fall
and rise
through life

Invitation

If
in the palm of your hand
you held it
would you know?
If
in the cool of the night
you felt it
could you tell?
After
long laying
in the arms of chaos
what would it take
for you
to recognize peace?
What would it take
for you
to settle softly?

Solace

My hope
is for these words
to embrace you
even as distance
sits
between us
and for love
to run
beside you
so you know
that you are never
alone

To any and everyone,

"May mercy, peace, and love be multiplied unto you."

~Jude 1:2

Lightning Source UK Ltd.
Milton Keynes UK
UKRC031946050123
414911UK00004B/13